my itty-bitty bio

Thomas Edison

Published in the United States of America by Cherry Lake Publishing
Ann Arbor, Michigan
www.cherrylakepublishing.com

Content Adviser: Ryan Emery Hughes, Doctoral Student, School of Education, University of Michigan
Reading Adviser: Marla Conn MS, Ed., Literacy specialist, Read-Ability, Inc.
Book Design: Jennifer Wahi
Illustrator: Jeff Bane

Photo Credits: ©Bardocz Peter/Shutterstock, 5; ©Everett Historical/Shutterstock, 7; ©Everett Collection/Shutterstock, 9; ©Paul Dempsey/Shutterstock, 11; ©Everett Historical/Shutterstock, 13; ©Everett Historical/Shutterstock, 15, 22; ©Everett Historical/Shutterstock, 17, 23; ©Khaled ElAdawy/Shutterstock, 19; ©Everett Historical/Shutterstock, 21; Cover, 8, 16, 18, Jeff Bane; Various frames throughout, ©Shutterstock Images

Library of Congress Cataloging-in-Publication Data

Names: Devera, Czeena, author.
Title: Thomas Edison / by Czeena Devera.
Description: Ann Arbor : Cherry Lake Publishing, [2018] | Series: My itty-bitty bio | Audience: Grades K to grade 3. | Includes bibliographical references and index.
Identifiers: LCCN 2018003114| ISBN 9781534128880 (hardcover) | ISBN 9781534130586 (pdf) | ISBN 9781534132085 (pbk.) | ISBN 9781534133785 (hosted ebook)
Subjects: LCSH: Edison, Thomas A. (Thomas Alva), 1847-1931--Juvenile literature. | Inventors--United States--Biography--Juvenile literature. | Electrical engineers--United States--Biography--Juvenile literature.
Classification: LCC TK140.E3 D48 2018 | DDC 621.3092 [B] --dc23
LC record available at https://lccn.loc.gov/2018003114

Printed in the United States of America
Corporate Graphics

table of contents

About the author: Czeena Devera grew up in the red-hot heat of Arizona surrounded by books. Her childhood bedroom had built-in bookshelves that were always too full. She now lives in Michigan with an even bigger library of books.

About the illustrator: Jeff Bane and his two business partners own a studio along the American River in Folsom, California, home of the 1849 Gold Rush. When Jeff's not sketching or illustrating for clients, he's either swimming or kayaking in the river to relax.

my story

I was born in Ohio in 1847. My family moved to Michigan seven years later.

WISCONSIN
St Paul
Eau Claire
Mississippi
Appleton
Rochester
Milwaukee
Madison
Rapids
Rockford
Davenport
ILLINOIS
Springfield
Lake Michigan
Grand Rapids
MICHIGAN
Lansing
Chicago
Gary
South Bend
Fort Wayne
INDIANA
Indianapolis
Toledo
Lake Huron
Toronto
Detroit
Lake Erie
Cleveland
Akron
Columbus
OHIO
Ohio
WEST VIRGINIA

We were poor. I had six brothers and sisters. I was the youngest.

How many siblings do you have?

I started my own newspaper at 14. Over 300 people used to buy it!

I liked to study things. But sometimes I made mistakes. I started a fire on a train. It was a mistake.

What do you do if you make a mistake?

I traveled the United States.
I worked as a **telegrapher**.
But I liked to invent more.

Where would you like to travel?

I invented the first **electronic** voting machine. It would have helped people vote faster. But no one wanted to use it yet.

I sold my first
invention in 1871.
I used the money to
open a **laboratory**.

I invented the first **phonograph**. I invented a way for everyone to light their homes.

I had 1,093 inventions before I died in 1931. I started an **electric** company. It still exists today.

What would you like to ask me?

timeline

1869

1840

Born 1847

1871

1950

Died
1931

glossary

electric (ih-LEK-trik) having to do with a form of energy called electricity

electronic (ih-lek-TRAH-nik) powered by a form of energy called electricity

invention (in-VEN-chuhn) some useful thing that is newly made

laboratory (LAB-ruh-tor-ee) a room or building that has special tools for scientists to use

phonograph (FOH-nuh-graf) a machine that plays record albums

telegrapher (TEL-ih-graf-ur) a person who uses a special system that sends messages over long distances

index